BUTTER

FOR

MARIE

Memoirs of My Liverpool

by

MARIE HANSON-CORDWELL

Co-writer

Velda Marie Laurie

Velda Marie Laurie

i

First published 1991 by Countyvise Limited, 1 & 3 Grove Road, Rock Ferry, Birkenhead, Wirral, Merseyside L42 3XS.

Copyright © Velda Marie Laurie, 1991.

Photoset and printed by Birkenhead Press Limited, 1 & 3 Grove Road, Rock Ferry, Birkenhead, Merseyside L42 3XS.

ISBN 0 907768 42 3.

DEDICATION

For

My Grandchildren

and

Great Grandchildren

With Love

FOREWORD

by

CILLA BLACK

It's really marvellous that somebody is recording their memories of the Liverpool of long ago. I'm sure it will be of great interest to future generations.

I wish this book every success and I'm sure it will be a valued addition to anyone's book collection.

Cilla Black

CONTENTS

Chapter   **Page**

1 The Beeches 1

2 Liverpool... 20

3 The Convent 25

4 On the Breadline................................ 31

5 The Home... 43

6 Charlie 55

7 Independence 60

8 Alder Hey Hospital........................... 63

9 Back to School................................. 68

10 My First Job.................................... 72

11 The Shop.. 76

12 Robert... 87

Epilogue.. 93

Chapter I

THE BEECHES

"Good gracious Mrs Hanson — fancy putting all that butter on your children's bread". Mrs Wordsworth's disapproval was apparent by her stance, and her large feathered hat seemed to shake and tremble like an outraged swan. She was very tall and angular, with an extremely large nose down which she looked with contempt at the world around her at all times. My Mamma continued to put plenty of butter on thin slices of bread whilst at the same time rebuking her antagonist, "Mrs Wordsworth, there may come a time when I can't afford to put butter on my children's bread, so in the meantime they shall have it in abundance".

Around that time it was very fashionable to have afternoon tea, and so Mrs Wordsworth continued to call on us, despite her admonishment. Mamma plainly did not like her visitor, who was very mean-natured and whose children were subjected to the severest discipline which almost amounted to cruelty. She and her husband owned a jewellery shop in a fashionable suburb of Birmingham, and as my father did a lot of business with the family mamma was forced to bear with her.

A lovely lady, Mrs Fraser, lived next door to us, and we were very fond of her. She had three sons, but no daughters, and dearly loved me to visit her on occasion. Her family always drank China tea, which my Mamma thought very insipid, although I adored it. Once, having failed to coax Mamma into buying

China tea, I decided to leave home and go and live next door. Mamma packed a small case for me and handed me over the fence, at the same time saying to Mrs Fraser: "For goodness sake don't give her mince pie, or she'll be very sick". I remember I stayed one whole day, being thoroughly spoiled, until towards the end of the evening Mrs Fraser said to me: "Marie, where are you going to sleep tonight? I don't have a spare bed for you". So I picked up my case and went back home in high dudgeon.

My father, George, was a business man with an office in New Street, Birmingham. He commuted by train, and the railway station at the bottom of our road was certainly an advantage because he was a hefty man, and walking even short distances caused him to puff and blow like a whale. I remember him as being tall, balding, and sporting a heavy moustache. He was always very smartly dressed and I can remember to this day the heavy gold chain which he wore across his girth.

Father loved good music and would sit listening for hours to our old gramophone, overcome with emotion, tears pouring down his cheeks. To this day I take after him in that respect. He must have been around forty-seven years old when he married Mamma, who was then in her early thirties. He was successful and lived well, never looking to the future even when he had a wife and three children.

Mamma's name was Anne and she was born and bred in Liverpool — the middle daughter of three. A tall, handsome woman, very upright in stature; she mostly attired herself in long velvet dresses, invariably trimmed with lace, and on outings she always wore large fashionable hats trimmed with

2

feathers or flowers. She had had a very sad upbringing; her parents lived only for drink, leaving their three small daughters to fend for themselves, and Mamma determined that she would marry well and that any children born to her would not have to face the hardships she and her sisters endured.

Mamma's eldest sister went into a nunnery as soon as she was old enough to be accepted; the youngest escaped from home by marrying when she was only seventeen, leaving Mamma, who eventually became the manageress of a large and famous chain of sweet and toffee shops. She was visiting one of the shops in this chain, in Birmingham, when she met my father, who had a very sweet tooth. He was already married when they met, but his wife was an alchoholic and he was unable to live with her. He had one son from that marriage, Jack, whom I hardly knew, although he was always around, somewhere in the background, a constant thorn in Mamma's side.

Being Mamma's first child of her liaison with my father, I came along before his wife died of her addiction to alcohol. They moved house as soon as I was born, and failed to register my birth. Fortunately they did have me baptised and my baptismal certificate is the only proof of my existence. I didn't find out about this situation until adulthood, when I applied for a passport, and at that time it caused me both concern and distress.

We lived in Sutton Coldfield on the outskirts of Birmingham in a large house in a very pleasant road. The house was beautifully and expensively furnished, and I vividly remember the splendid grandfather clock, the gorgeous marble fire-surround and the French windows in the drawing room which led onto a lovely garden. My brother George and I both inherited father's deep love of gardening and of everything that grows. But father had another passion — women — and there was more trouble in our house over women than anything else.

Now and then rumours would filter through to Mamma that father was having an affair with one of his secretaries. On these occasions, she would dress me nicely and take me with her to father's office. She would burst in on him in a towering rage, and the secretary, innocent or otherwise, would scuttle away fast leaving father to pacify Mamma as best he could.

When he had quietened her down he would usually take us off to the market where he would down whole oysters, refusing me any, saying I would be sick. On other occasions, he would take us to a smart cafe for afternoon tea and cakes. Wherever he went he always wore a tea rose in his lapel, and I always cried for one, in vain.

After these excursions Mamma and I would go home, having extracted a promise from father that he would be home early. He never was, and Mamma would keep me up late making wild accusations against him, which I never understood. She would then take me up to their bedroom, undress me and put me in the middle of their bed. I loved their room because there was a light outside and a laburnam tree which made pretty patterns on the wall. Father would eventually come home and there would be high words downstairs. On coming up to bed he would find me there and say: "What is Marie doing here?", and Mamma would say "You know why she's here". All very mystifying to a little girl!

Father always resented me because I was the reason he had to marry again. Had Mamma not become pregnant with me he would probably have been quite content to have gone from one lady to another. However, he adored my sister, Patsy, who was born in wedlock, so I used to do many things I thought were clever, just to please him.

From an early age I was an avid reader, and I remember well one Saturday lunchtime, having just finished reading one of my many children's books I greeted father as he came through the front door, with a deep curtsy, saying: "Good morning Mr Cow", a quote from my newly-read book. I was preparing to continue the little verse when I felt my bottom being well and truly tanned. Mamma had taken exception to my little performance and I was delegated to the kitchen to have lunch with the maid. I heard father ask Mamma what I had done to invoke such wrath, and she said I had called him a cow. I would only have been about five years old at the time and was just showing off.

I was educated privately by two old-maid school teachers, who in fact taught me very little, and much of my education throughout all my school days came from books I read.

We grew up not knowing our grandparents on either side of the family, but Mamma kept in touch with her younger sister, Jane, who lived in Liverpool, and every year we would have two weeks holiday in New Brighton on the opposite side of the Mersey — that is Patsy and me, our little brother, George, Mamma and the maid. Aunt Jane would then come across from Liverpool on the ferry with our cousins to join us.

Mamma with me

Mamma with Marie, Patsy and George

Mamma & Father

Father with his business colleagues – second front left

New Brighton was completely unspoiled in those days and we revelled in those holidays — the donkey rides, the sea and sand, and the sun which always seemed to shine, enchanted us. But not father. He hated New Brighton with a fierce intensity, but would be forced to visit us at least once while we were there or Mamma would threaten to go back home, accusing him of having another woman there, which was probably true.

On the day of father's visit we would all troop down to meet him at the ferry, and Mamma would arrange for him to have a beach-basket chair and the latest novel. Despite all this pampering he would quickly tire of the scene and would commence moaning and groaning about how he hated it, and pleading with Mamma to arrange for us all to take a coach trip around the pretty Wirral countryside. She would say: "No George, you need the rest, and you know driving always makes Marie feel sick". I can't ever remember being travel-sick, but some excuse had to be made to keep him there and I always seemed to be the scapegoat in those days, one way or another.

Later in the year father and Mamma would spend their annual holiday on the Continent, without us children, leaving us in the care of the maid.

I loved the summers in our garden where we often had tea under the elderflower tree. I used to try to help father in the garden, and remember his astonishment one day when I refused to pick up a worm off the garden path, even for a silver sixpence, which was a princely sum in those days. Needless to say, my sister, Patsy, obliged, as she always loved to upstage me. Patsy was then a very destructive child who would break her own things and then go on to destroy my treasures, and I sometimes found it difficult to form an affectionate relationship with her.

Our maid at that time, Sarah, regularly took us to the rather large and lovely park which was close to home. One day Mamma went to meet father in Birmingham, alone, and knowing that the territorials were encamped in the park she told Sarah to keep us at home. I didn't know anything about this, but as soon as Mamma had gone, Sarah put on our coats and we were away to the park, where she had high jinks with the soldier boys.

When Mamma was putting us to bed that night she asked what we had been doing that afternoon, and very excitedly I told her we had been to see the soldier boys in the park. She promptly had screaming hysterics and demanded that father take Sarah back home to her parents immediately, which he had no option but to do. I think if father had not immediatley done as he was told, Mamma would have struck the girl. Poor Sarah; I was sorry to see her go because she told us quite marvelous ghost stories which filled us with both terror and delight. Sadly, she was only one of the many victims of Mamma's towering rages.

Mamma was truly afraid of thunder, and the day after Sarah left she developed what she called a 'thundery headache' and sent me off to the chemist for some tablets. The thunder was already starting to rumble as I left the house and I hurried up the hill as fast as my legs would carry me. As I left the chemist shop the rain was sheeting down, and within seconds my cotton dress was drenched through. The storm tnen broke violently above my head, and I was absolutely terrified. I saw a young couple just going into their house and I fell on them screaming, pleading with them to take me in. The young woman asked where I lived, and when I told her she said: "Good gracious little girl, that's not far for you to go. Run along now". So for the first time in my life I lost some faith in human nature.

When I did arrive home it was to find all the curtains drawn and Mamma crouched in a corner, huddled over Patsy and George. A minute or two later father came puffing in exclaiming: "I knew I would find you in this state Anne — pull yourself together woman and consider what you are doing to your children". Then he went off to make some tea, and in fact that was the only occasion I can ever remember him making tea, as he was firmly of the opinion that tea-making was the prerogotive of the female of the species.

My step-brother, Jack, badly wanted a dog. Father said "Yes" and Mamma said "No — if a dog comes into this house then I go out of it".

Despite Mamma's protestations, a little brown dog arrived at "The Beeches" one Friday evening. It had no particular pedigree, but he seemed a friendly little chap, and we decided to call him Prince. Sadly he only lasted the weekend with us. All day Saturday Mamma did her best to avoid Prince, but if he did go anywhere near her she would scream in terror, frightening the poor little dog almost as much as she herself was terrified by it.

On the Sunday, father put a lead on Prince and told Patsy, George and me to take him for a walk, while Jack was at Church. So off we went — not very happy about it. Half-way down the next street Prince decided to go for a gallop, we three holding on to him like grim death. He finally pulled us over, and not daring to let go of the lead we were dragged along the road, screaming. Eventually a lady came out of her house, took charge of the situation and returned us home. What a sorry sight we were! Our hand-knitted stockings were in ribbons, as were our white starched dresses, and there was blood everywhere.

When Jack came home from Church he was told to return Prince from whence he came, and from that day the animosity between Mamma and Jack grew greater and greater until he eventually joined the Army — a Cavalry Division I believe — to get away from it all.

Mamma was also terrified of cows, and she once told me that whilst on holiday in Stratford-Upon-Avon with father and another couple, before I was born, they were walking in the countryside with the two gentlemen in front and the ladies a short distance behind, when a farmer let his herd of cows out of the field. The cows were between the ladies and the gentlemen, and Mamma went completely hysterical and actually went down on her knees and prayed to the farmer to take them away. Apparently he responded by putting his hands on his hips and laughing at her. Father eventually realised what was happening, and rushing back he belaboured the farmer with his walking stick.

Poor Mamma — her fear of dogs, cows and thunder remained with her for life. I suppose some of her fears rubbed off on me as I always stayed well away from dogs and cows until I became adult, and I did not overcome my fear of thunder until the Blitz of World War 2, that was to come. I did, however, make a solemn promise to myself that if ever I had children of my own I would never show those fears, and I'm proud to say I kept that promise.

One day a young woman arrived at our house accompanied by a little girl of about two years old. Father was very embarrassed and cross. After a while the young woman went away, bathed in tears, leaving the little girl behind. Mamma, who was pregnant herself at the time, said we had a new sister! Poor little one — she cried night and day for her own mother, and after about three days the young woman returned and took her away. Of course it was father in trouble again, this time with proof of one of his infidelities.

About this time he had a short spell in hospital with kidney problems and his doctor advised him to retire or he would end up in a wheelchair. Of course he could not afford to retire because he spent his money as he earned it, on the good things of life. Also, there was now a fourth addition to his young family, a baby boy called Dennis.

Father was a very abstemious man, never known to finish a glass of beer. However, our cellar was always well-stocked for his friends and business colleagues. He was a great raconteur with a ready wit, and because of this he was very popular at his many Clubs, where he often arranged the entertainment. He loved to recite poetry and would often entertain his friends this way.

After his illness father started to slow up and to worry about money. Nevertheless he continued to go to his clubs and functions, but refused to buy Mamma a new hat. It was beginning to dawn on him that he was almost fifty-four years old, overweight, and not in the best of health.

On Christmas Day 1913 we spent the day with family friends, and it was to be many years before I again saw a decorated Christmas tree that reached the ceiling. I remember that father bought Mamma, Patsy and me a set of matching rolled-gold bracelets, rings and necklets that year. I didn't have mine very long because after chewing up her own set my sister, Patsy, proceeded to chew up mine. They were delicate and fragile, so it was easily done.

One Saturday lunchtime at the beginning of the year 1914 father came home from his office looking most upset. He walked into the kitchen, where he sat down heavily on a rocking chair; once again we were between maids or he would have gone straight into the dining room. Spreading the morning papers across his knees he looked sadly at Mamma and said: "Anne, I hope to God I am not around when England and Germany go to war, as they most certainly will".

In the early spring of that same year, baby Dennis became very ill with what was then known as Infantile Paralysis. Now, of course, we call it Poliomyelitis. I can't remember how long he was ill, but sadly, nothing could be done for him and Mamma said the Virgin Mary and the angels were coming to take him to heaven.

I can see Dennis now in his little coffin, laid on a beautiful oval inlaid table. Father looked down at his baby son, and turning to Mamma said: "That is where I will be very soon Anne". A few weeks later, shortly after his fifty-fourth birthday, his words came true. He was at a social evening for the Society of Yorkshire Folk in Birmingham, and was on stage doing what he loved best, reciting a poem called 'The Dream' when he suddenly put out a hand towards Mamma and said: "Anne, I'm falling", which he proceeded to do. Mamma rushed to his side and he was brought home unconcious. This was a Saturday, and he lived only until the following Wednesday.

Before he died Mamma took Patsy, George and me into the bedroom where he lay — not recognising us — to say goodbye to him. I asked her: "How do people die?" and she answered: "Oh, they just stop breathing". Very forcefully I said: "Well, I won't stop breathing". Then Jack arrived to say goodbye, and a little while later, while we young ones were in the kitchen, he came down the stairs to tell us father had died. At that I took hold of Patsy and George by their hands and said: "Come along, let us all die" and we went out into the garden where we were eventually discovered by Mrs Wordsworth banging our heads against the wall. She asked us what we were doing and I answered that we were trying to die, like father. She promptly took us back indoors to Mamma and told her what we had been doing, and then she took Patsy and me back home with her, where we stayed until after the funeral was over, and where we were very miserable being constantly chastised, as were her own children, just for being normal little girls, or so I thought. Mamma kept little George with her for company.

When we returned home it was to find that Mamma had dispensed with the services of the maid.

She told us we were going to live in Liverpool, a City where little children were so poor they had no shoes on their feet and wore old rags to keep them warm. She also told us that a lot of grown-up people in Liverpool were drunkards, and sometimes not very clean — facts which amazed us, and which turned out to be only too true.

Knowing that Mamma was an astute business-woman, father's friends did their best to persuade her to stay in Birmingham, offering to set her up in business, but sadly she could not be persuaded, saying she would be better off amongst her own people in her home town.

Hectic days followed with Mamma packing and Jack clamouring for as many of father's belongings he could get. He was engaged to be married at that time, but Mamma insisted that he paid for what he wanted, saying she had three children to rear and could not afford to give anything away.

When father's Will was read we discovered that all he had left was the sum of £300, some beautiful jewellery and some fine furniture.

When the obituary appeared in the newspaper it was plain he had never acknowledged me as his child for it stated he had left a wife and two young children, a third child having died a few weeks previously.

The day before we moved to Liverpool we visited father's grave and I helped Mamma to plant pansies on it. The next time I saw it I was in my early twenties and accompanied by my husband. The cemetery was greatly enlarged and the grave was surrounded by many new ones. Whilst on this sentimental journey I went to see my old home in Coleshill Road, Sutton Coldfield. I stood outside for a while and the memories came flooding back — the name was still on the gate "The Beeches", and the front garden was exactly as I remembered it. I looked at my darling husband with tears in my eyes — he squeezed my hand and said: "You should never look back love".

The day after Mamma and I planted the pansies a huge van came to take all our belongings away to be stored in Liverpool until we found somewhere to settle. We followed by train, which was very exciting, for me at least — crossing the Mersey over the Runcorn Bridge, and then the bustle of Lime Street Station.

I was just seven years old that bitterly cold March day of 1914. War was just around the corner, and unknowingly I had left behind the years of my childhood, and became an adult.

George's Landing Stage

Chapter II

LIVERPOOL

Liverpool — City of my childish dreams. Dirty, but magnificent, and with a heart of gold. I was to make it my home for 65 years and will never call myself anything other than a Liverpudlian no matter where I live, and despite the heartaches of the early years spent there.

At Lime Street Station we hailed a cab which took us through some of the back streets of Liverpool where the air of abject poverty was apparent, and brought home to me Mamma's earlier tales of Liverpool which until then I had half considered to be no more than fairy stories. Undernourished, dirty little children were playing in the streets, barefoot. Garbage spilled over the pavements and the smell was quite dreadful even from the inside of our taxi-cab.

We were going to live with Mamma's sister, Jane, and her husband Tom, who managed a public house on the corner of a street called Springfield. If ever there was a misnomer it was this street, which was situated in one of the worst slum areas of the City.

The cabbie pulled up outside the Springfield Public House, and as we were heaving our luggage into the premises an incident occurred which made a profound impression on me, which still remains. Two small girls passed by, barefoot and ragged, sharing a currant bun between them. Suddenly one of them gave a shout, exclaiming: "Oh Lottie, you've dropped a currant", at which Lottie turned around, picked up the currant and ate it. Until then I had no knowledge of the pangs of hunger, but I was soon to learn.

Uncle Tom ushered us through the bar and up the stairs into the living quarters. Every room we were shown was very dirty; the complete opposite of everthing we had previously known, and an awful smell of beer drifting up from the public house below pervaded everywhere.

In the dining room a table was set for tea, and in the centre of it, to our horror, stood an open tin of condensed milk covered with flies. I was totally lost for words and could only manage a wan smile when I was fussed over and kissed by Aunt Jane and Uncle Tom, whilst Patsy and George clung to Mamma wide-eyed and startled.

Uncle Tom was a big, domineering man with a dictatorial manner, whilst Aunt Jane was a kind, sweet, downtrodden person who never disputed anything Uncle Tom said because in his eyes he was always right. They had four children: two girls, Dolly and Bunty, who were around my age, and two boys, the older one whose name was Fred, and a baby of about nine months old, Tony, who was sitting in a rickety old high chair.

Our older cousins stood around gazing in wonder at us standing there in our smart clothes, and suddenly, possibly overwhelmed by all the visitors the baby started to cry. At this, Aunt Jane scooped the flies of the top of the condensed milk with a spoon, after which she dipped the baby's dummy in it and gave it to him to suck.

Worse was to come. At bedtime I was asked to share a big bed in a tiny room with my two girl cousins. I didn't mind this too much until I discovered that the bedlinen was infested with bed-bugs, which my cousins totally ignored but which filled me with terror. I decided to sleep at the bottom of the bed underneath an old coat, and I scratched and itched all night long.

Dolly and Bunty had their fun before they settled down to sleep that first night, calling into their brother Fred's bedroom and demanding that he display his 'willy'. They giggled and shrieked, and their laughter was so infectious that I joined in, although for the life of me I couldn't see what all the fuss was about since I had regularly helped Mamma to bathe my little brother, George, and was quite familiar with, and unimpressed by the difference between the sexes. Although I did wonder if cousin Fred had something my young brother didn't have. In any event, he refused to oblige his sisters that first night, saying he was not going to show it off in front of me. Several nights later he did succumb to their blandishments and displayed this famous 'willy', and although I feigned interest and laughed along with Dolly and Bunty, I was really not impressed.

The day after we moved into our temporary home Mamma did a little judicious cleaning around the living quarters whilst awaiting the return of Aunt Jane and Uncle Tom from their work in the public house. Later that same evening all three of them sat down to discuss our future, and Mamma decided she would like to open a shop, which certainly met with Aunt Jane and Uncle Tom's approval.

So Mamma commenced her search for a suitable business, and after a couple of weeks found what she wanted at a price she could afford. It was to be a general shop at the corner of Greenwood Terrace; another misnomer of a street, but a fairly good environmental change for the better.

Before moving into our new home we had to spend several more rather miserable weeks in Aunt Jane and Uncle Tom's rather squalid home. The kitchen was the worst; tea-towels sent up from the bar to be washed remained in a pile on the floor, and still unwashed were used to dry our dishes. The food offered was adequate, but we all found it difficult to eat because of the lack of hygiene in the surroundings, which we were totally unused to. We never had fresh milk; it was always the inevitable condensed milk or 'Conny-Onny' as it was affectionately called.

In the course of the next two weeks I developed a violent toothache and Uncle Tom elected to pull the offending tooth out to save the cost of a bill at the dentist. I will never forget the feel of his fat, beery fingers moving around my mouth as he wrapped a piece of strong thread around the aching tooth, after which he tied the other end to the knob of the bedroom door and slammed the door shut. The tooth did come out, and after the awful pain of the extraction had settled down the toothache disappeared.

Eventually the day came when Mamma, Patsy, little George and I moved to our new home. Our furniture came out of store and moved in with us, except for the few pieces which my half-brother, Jack, had kept. My lovely piano was there and Mamma decided I should have lessons from the music teacher at the end of the road. Sadly, I was not able to keep them up, and have regretted it ever since.

When the question of our education came up for discussion Mamma said she could easily manage, but Uncle Tom said of course she could not and that Patsy and I would be better educated in a convent than in one of the local schools, and then Mamma would only have young George to contend with while she got on with the business of running the shop. Initially she was against the idea, but was eventually won over, so that a couple of weeks after moving into our new home Patsy and I entered a convent in a rather salubrious part of Liverpool, in the direction of Southport.

And so began one of the most terrifying periods of our childhood.

Chapter III

THE CONVENT

The Sunday Patsy and I entered the convent was one of the most distressing days of my young life. Mamma and Aunt Jane accompanied us, and as it was Benediction time we were immediately separated from them and ushered into a line of girls waiting to go into Church.

Patsy screamed, and tears were not far from my own eyes, but Mamma had given me a good talking to, telling me I was a big girl now and must look after Patsy, learn my lessons and be good. So we were marched into the Church, with Patsy screaming after Mamma and me doing my best to pacify her. I was also fearful, because I had previously led a very sheltered life, mixing with few people, and now it seemed I was surrounded by hundreds of hostile strangers.

How we got through the rest of that day I don't remember, but fortunately we were allocated beds in the same dormitory. During the first night, after I had quietly cried myself to sleep, I was awakened by a Nun, who in her long black robes presented a terrifying sight to me; she had apparently been trying to make Patsy stop crying, and was on the verge of slapping her. The Nun allowed me to climb into bed with my sister, givig her what comfort I could until we both slept from sheer exhaustion and misery.

I can't remember what we had to eat for breakfast, but I know we had to go into a very large room called the Refectory and because of the difference in our ages Patsy and I were not allowed to sit together at the same table.

After breakfast we were all asked if we had been to the toilet, and I later learned that if we needed to go during lesson times we would be forced to use a bucket which was placed behind a large screen on a raised platform, where we could be heard by everyone in the class. When I questioned this I was told that a request to go to the toilet during lesson times was a venal sin for which God would punish us severely.

I was already able to read and write when I entered the Convent, but I was not allowed to continue my studies at that point and had to start learning right from the bottom, making pot hooks with a slate and pencil. I was very upset about this, but the teaching-nun said I had to do these things whether I liked it or not, to please God.

Each afternoon after lessons were over we were all ushered into a tiny room, bare of furniture, which, looking back, reminded me of tales of The Black Hole of Calcutta. When we had all been crowded into this room, one of the maids would enter with a laundry basket full of end-crusts from the day's bread, spread with margarine. There was never enough for every girl to have a piece, but the maid would throw the crusts around and those who failed to catch a piece had to ask for a share of someone else's. This was supposed to take the edge off our appetites before tea-time.

After tea we had prayers, and then, if the weather was fine we were allowed out into the grounds, which were surrounded by a very high wall. Oh how we yearned to be the other side of it! If the weather was inclement we stayed indoors and sang nursery rhymes.

Sadly, I failed to make a single friend whilst I was at the Convent, mainly because most of my spare time was taken up in caring for Patsy, and when we were together she would be clinging to me, bathed in tears.

When the Sisters discovered I was seven years old they decided it was time I took my first Holy Communion, so I had to attend special religious classes. I did my very best to believe what the nuns and priests told me about God, and very much enjoyed hearing about the Miracles, hoping such things might offer me a way out. I prayed hard that a Miracle would bring father back and let us return to our old happy life, and since my prayers were so fervent I could not understand why God didn't hear them and do something about it. Wasn't he supposed to be a kind and loving God who heard our prayers and attended to all our needs?

It became even harder for me to believe in the teachings of the Church when I was indoctrinated in the belief that hellfire and brimstone awaited me if ever I dared to take one step out of line.

When the time came for me to take my first confession I was unable to think of a single sin worthy of the confessional, so that when I did actually enter that dreadful, dark, box-like place I made up the most horrific sins I could possibly think of. What the priest thought I never knew, but he was a youngish man with a pleasant face, and he smiled at me kindly after he had given me his blessing.

Parents were invited to witness our first Communion, and I can remember there was a dreadful storm between Mamma and the Sister-in-Charge over the dress I should wear. Mamma had arranged to have a beautiful dress in a pale cream colour with a blue sash specially made for me, but the Sister insisted that the dress should be white. Mamma said she had spent a lot of money on our uniforms and that she could not afford another dress, and, although the sister carried on alarmingly, Mamma stuck to her guns and I wore the cream dress.

After the Ceremony we all sat down to a special breakfast; the only substantial meal I can remember having whilst at the Convent.

After our first term two very subdued little girls went home for the end-of-term holiday, which sadly, was not a happy time. Young as I was I realised that things were going badly with the shop, and apart from that the country was on the brink of war and everyone was very jittery and unsettled.

Mamma herself was a changed person; worn out with worry and more than ever inclined to fly into a temper. Despite this I would much rather have stayed at home with her than return to the terrifying cloisters of the Convent. But this was not to be, and at the end of the holiday she handed Patsy and me a bag of sweets each, at the same time telling us we were taking all of her profits, and back we went.

Day after day the Holy Sisters tried to drum into us that God was a loving, caring person, and that our sins would be punished by eternal hellfire. Even at my tender age I could not reconcile the two, and in my young heart I firmly believed that if anyone deserved punishment it was the Holy Sisters themselves for their appalling treatment of, and uncaring attitude to little children, and, most of all for planting such unimaginable fears and terrors into their childish minds. How very different they were from today's loving and caring Sisterhood of the Catholic Church.

Shortly after returning from our end-of-term holiday my sister's health began to fail. Generally speaking Patsy was a much stronger and more robust child than I was, but she succumbed to a debilitating illness, suffering acute attacks of diarrhoea and becoming unable to eat anything at all.

My heart almost broke as I witnessed her being continually slapped on her bare bottom for soiling her bedsheets, when it should have been obvious she was far too ill to walk, let alone go to the toilet without assistance. Ill as she was, no doctor was called in. She was merely kept in bed in the 'care' of the maids-of-all-work, and at times they were almost as callous as the Holy Sisters themselves.

At this time I developed a sore throat and my mouth and throat were covered in ulcers. When I complained to the Sisters about my condition they told me I had obviously been behaving badly, and it would only get better when I behaved better for God.

Fortunately we were allowed to write one letter home every two weeks, so I wrote to Mamma telling her how things were with us. She came to the Convent post haste, and despite the Holy Sister's reluctance to allow it, she demanded to see us, and when she did, the sight of her two desperately sick little daughters sent her into one of her towering rages. Her tongue-lashing must have put the Holy Sisters, and the rest of the staff, in fear and trembling of hellfire and brimstone for eternity.

When she had had her say, Mamma gathered us up, took us home and put us to bed. She then sent for the doctor, who was horrified at our condition, and it took several weeks before either of us regained our health and strength, despite the care and nurturing we received.

I don't know if any reports were levelled at the authorities, but much to our relief Patsy and I never returned to the hated Convent.

Chapter IV

ON THE BREADLINE

In due course Patsy and I recovered and were found places at the local school, St. Michael's, where we were much happier than we had been at the Convent. But poor Mamma — her real troubles were only just beginning — now she had three of us to look after as well as managing the shop. Then war broke out; the very thing father never wanted to live to see — he had his wish in that respect.

Things went from bad to worse at the shop. Mamma let out too much credit and never got paid back. She was forced to sell some of our cherished furniture, the grandfather clock being the first to go.

We three children contracted every childish ailment imaginable — measles, chickenpox, whooping cough; it seemed that at least one of us was always ill with something or another.

Mamma often talked of killing herself, striking terror into our hearts. All her troubles would pour out to me, being the eldest, and although I did not fully comprehend the enormity of her problems I knew that it helped her to talk to me about them.

I took a good deal of solace in my father's books, which we had brought with us, and by the time I was nine years old I had read War and Peace twice, not having understood any of it the first time and very little of it at the second attempt. Nevertheless it fascinated me.

Eventually we decided to take in a lodger to try to help things out financially. He was an elderly man, and hardly ever sober, which Mamma could not abide. Consequently she did her best to keep Patsy, George and me well out of his way. One day, in utter desperation, she sold the shop to this man for the paltry sum of £100, and then we had to look for somewhere else to live.

We eventually found rooms in a basement, with a stone floor which always felt cold and damp, whatever the weather. Our quarters consisted of a living room containing a fire-place with oven, one large bedroom and a wash-house. The house itself was very big and was owned by an old harridan who lived on the premises and who threatened us with eviction if we made the slightest sound. All the other rooms were rented out to lodgers, who dare not miss a single week's rent or they would find their belongings out in the street and the door locked against them.

Mamma and her £100 were soon parted because there were still a few bills outstanding from the shop, and we all needed new warm clothing.

The next thing was to find a new school for Patsy and me, and we were eventually enrolled at St. Francis Xavier's. Then Mamma found herself an occasional job which took her out of the house at all sorts of odd hours of the day, and sometimes the night. While she was out at work I was left in charge of Patsy and George, and I would do my best to look after them, helping them to wash and dress, and giving them meals.

Mamma continued to cry over our changed circumstances, saying she should have taken father's friends advice and remained in Birmingham — but that was all too late. Some days she could barely afford to feed us, and she continued to pour out all her troubles to me so that at eight years of age I had a very old head on my young shoulders. She was forced to sell our lovely mahogany bureau for a few pounds, and then she started taking all her precious jewellery to the pawn shop; that was the last she saw of it because she never had enough money to redeem the pledge.

One black winter's night, when Mamma was particularly tearful, she found she had only two pennies left to her name and we had nothing in the house for tea. Shops stayed open until quite late in those days and she told me to take a dish and go down the street to the little grocer's shop for two pennyworth of jam. That night is still a poignant memory, and to this day stands out vividly in my mind, because of Mamma's total despair which weighed heavily on me. Searchlights were flashing in the sky looking for enemy aircraft, and being a nervous child I was very fearful. I stopped in a doorway, sank down to my knees and prayed hard for a miracle, pleading with God once again to send father back to us, thinking it would solve all our problems. Subconciously I knew it could never be, and I sobbed bitter tears for us all.

The following day Mamma took her treasured wedding ring to the pawnbrokers, and we were all desolate, but as it happened that very same day she got herself a job in a munitions factory and it seemed our luck had changed for the better. The job meant that she would have to do shift work, including night work, and although she and I were worried at the idea of her being away from us throughout the night we knew our very livelihood depended on it. Mamma

Woman working in a Liverpool ammunitions factory

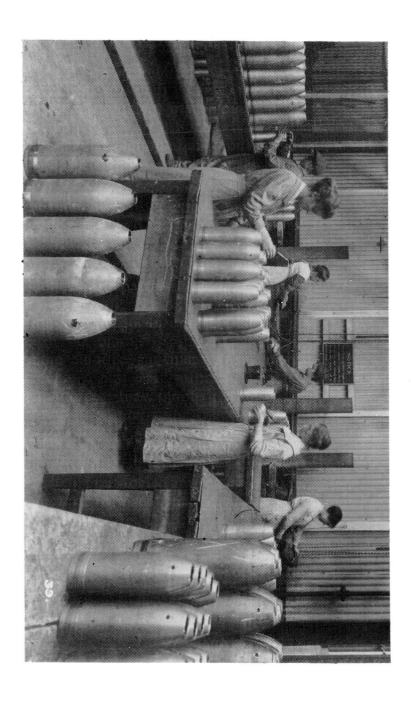

Women working in a Liverpool ammunitions factory

also worried about the other lodgers' drinking habits and was afraid they would disturb us, or even molest us — but it had to be done; she needed that job to keep us from starving.

On top of all our other problems, I never seemed to feel very well in myself and was forever complaining of toothache, headache, or just feeling nauseous.

After a particularly bad night spent with the toothache it was decided to send me to the dentist the following morning. The dentist said I had no bad teeth and he considered I was suffering from neuralgia and should go to see a doctor. When I told Mamma this she said she didn't believe I had been to the dentist at all, and so she took me back to him. The dentist said to her: "I saw this little girl this morning — there's nothing wrong with her teeth — she needs to see a doctor". So we walked along the road to the doctor's house, and after he had given me a cursory examination he told Mamma I was anaemic and would benefit from having a bottle of stout each night. He also said that my strength was all in my hair, which reached to my waist, and should consequently be cut off. Mamma did no such thing! Stout she could not afford, so she bought Parrish's Food, a popular iron tonic in those days, and over the years I took so much of it that it rotted my teeth, which had apparently been perfectly good until then.

Each time I went to see this particular doctor, complaining of feeling ill, he would say the same thing — that I was anaemic and only a nightly bottle of stout and having my hair cut would cure me. He was an elderly man with a beautiful little daughter, whose portrait hung in his surgery. His young wife had died, so he had married his housekeeper in order to have someone to look after the little girl, whom he idolised. However, he was seldom sober, and could often be seen staggering along the road demanding that his daughter and his wife walk several paces behind him, as befitted his station.

If the weather was good during the school holidays, and if we could afford it, we would meet up with Aunt Jane and our cousins, walk to the Pier Head and take the ferryboat across the Mersey to Seacombe. This was much cheaper than travelling the whole distance by ferry to New Brighton, which was our destination, but it meant that on arrival at Seacombe we would have a walk of about four miles along the coast road to get there. Once there, we would have a picnic lunch, and maybe a halfpenny cornet of ice cream, if funds ran to it. So very different from our earlier holidays when father was alive, but nevertheless it was a treat, and we enjoyed it.

After spending the day at New Brighton we would make the long trek back to Seacombe to get on the ferry which would take us across the Mersey to Liverpool. From there we had rather a long walk home, which was all uphill, but I really enjoyed that walk back because we went along Liverpool's then notorious Scotland Road, which was a wondrous sight to me. There, the ladies of Liverpool could be seen in their warm plaid shawls, striped Lindsay skirts and clean white aprons. For some reason, which was never explained to me, they were called Mary Ellens, and I was fascinated by the way they were able to fold their arms across their chests and at the same time balance large baskets on their heads, filled with either washing or fruit and vegetables.

Seacombe Ferry and Landing Stage

c. 1930 starboard view of ferry boat "Wallasey".

They had coarse mannerisms, but hearts of gold, and I loved them.

Gangs of young people would stand around, singing, and generally enjoying themselves, and Mamma would hurry us past saying: "Don't listen to them — they're common". I wonder what she would have thought of our darling Cilla Black, who came from that very area of Liverpool!

Also in Scotland Road was a confectioner's shop called Delaney's, who sold the most delicious Eccles cakes, and if Mamma could afford she would buy some for tea, which made our day complete.

Mamma always tried to keep up her genteel air, and in fact she succeeded, and insisted that we children were polite and well-spoken at all times. We did not take long to lose our slight Birmingham 'twang' and strangely enough we never did acquire a 'scouse' accent. In fact to this very day anyone who asks where I come from is surprised when I say: "from Liverpool", and I always say it with pride.

Mamma had a pleasant soprano voice, and as our old gramophone had long-since been sold-off, as had my lovely piano, she sometimes used to sing to us as she sat in front of the fire, while I brushed her hair, until she finally fell asleep. Her work in the munitions factory was hard, and she was often tired out when she came back home, and the stress of having to leave us alone when she was on night shift did not help. Her pay was poor, but it helped to clothe and feed us, although her health must have suffered in consequence.

She happened to be on night shift on New Year's Eve, 1916, so she put us to bed before going off to work. However, the noise of the people in the street celebrating the New Year woke me up and I thought it must be time to go to school. I jumped out of bed thinking we would be late, roused Patsy and George, washed and dressed them hurriedly and gave them some breakfast. Then we took ourselves off to school. I thought nothing of the fact that it was still dark, because in those days, at that time of the year, it was always dark when we set off for school. Naturally we found the school closed, and we returned home, only to be stopped by the old harridan who owned the house as we were going through the front door. She demanded an explanation as to why we were out walking the streets at that hour, and said she would speak to Mamma about it. I told Mamma myself what had happened and she was very upset, but not cross with me.

We had neither gaslight nor electricity in our rented rooms, and used candles for lighting purposes, which was something else that worried Mamma. One day she was asleep on the sofa, a few nights after the New Year's Eve incident, when Patsy took a lighted candle into a cubbyhole to look for something to play with. As usual, I had my head buried in a book, and didn't immediately notice that Patsy had leaned over the candle and set fire to herself. Then our combined screams woke Mamma, who rushed over to Patsy and put out the flames. I was at the top of the stairs by this time, and when she caught up with me, saying: "Where are you going?" I told her I was going to get the fire engine. She took me back downstairs and told me that if ever I came across anyone who was on fire in future, I was to wrap a rug or a coat around the person to extinguish the flames. Fortunately Patsy came to no harm herself, although she had burned a large hole in the front of her dress. However, we were all very upset, and Mamma said she could no longer cope, and that something must be done.

We were very subdued for a few days, and then the blow fell. Mamma sat us down and told us we would have to go into a Home, and in the meantime she would be able to save some money and look around for a little house, and then we would be able to come back to her. This was a bitter blow to me. I had done my best, but I realised Patsy could have burned to death had Mamma not been there to put the flames out, and also that anything could have happened to us while we were out on the streets on New Year's Eve. But I was still only a little girl.

Mamma went ahead with arrangements to put all three of us into a Home, and eventually found one halfway between where we were living at that time and our current school. "At least you won't have to change schools again" she told us "and I'll be able to visit you now and then, and it won't be for long — just until I find somewhere nice for us to live, somewhere we can really call home instead of sharing a house with all sorts of strange people". The Home Mamma found was run by a small Catholic Society and consisted of three large houses — one for babies, one for girls and one for boys. Patsy and I were to remain there until just after the war.

Chapter V

THE HOME

The Home was situated in one of the poorer districts of Liverpool, and even from the outside looked dreary and forbidding. Once inside, the air of poverty, overhanging the smell of institutional carbolic, made my stomach turn over.

There were about fifty boys housed in the boy's section, but I don't remember ever having seen the master in charge of them, so I cannot be a judge of his character. There were twenty-four girls in the girl's section, which was run by two spinsters who were, looking back, extremely embittered.

The nurse in charge of the babies' wing was a kind, loving person, and the babies were fortunate in being able to remain in her care until they were about four years old. Nurse Lee, for that was her name, obviously had a lot of love to give, and during my period at the Home she adopted a three-year-old orphan, a little girl whom she called Bonny Mary. Sadly, Bonny Mary died of tonsilitus when she was four and I remember we were all taken to her funeral.

Patsy and I both did our best to settle in at the Home, but my little brother George was the main problem this time. He had never been separated from Mamma before and could not cope with the rough and tumble of the boy's section. He was constantly bullied and teased by the other boys and kept on beating his little fists on the communicating door between the boys' house and ours, crying for me. I would try to console him through the locked door, but after a few weeks of this I was forced to ask Mamma to take him back home, which she did. This gave me a better chance to cope with the situation in which Patsy and I found oursleves.

The two spinster ladies in charge of our section were called Miss Martha, who was the Matron, and Miss Tilly, who was her assistant. Most of the children were orphans, and some of them had never known parents. Consequently they grew up in an atmosphere of neglect and maltreatment.

Tubercular glands in the neck were common among the girls, and although the sufferers were occasionally taken to see a doctor, all he did for them was to bandage up their necks, which continued to suppurate despite this attention. Eventually they were unable to hold their heads up at all and walked around with them lolling on one side — a sight which grieved me greatly.

Miss Tilly, the assistant Matron, never liked me; partly, I think, because I had a mother whom I could see regularly, and to whom I could complain when necessary. Sadly, when I did complain, Mamma was not able to take too much notice because there was absolutely nothing she could do about it at that time. On reflection it must have distressed her greatly.

The cleaning of the large girls' house was carried out by the girls themselves. My duties included polishing the huge staircase, which had beautiful banisters in rich mahogany, and also the wooden floor of a large hallway. On top of this I shared duties with other girls, looked after Patsy, and attended school, so that by the end of each day I usually felt totally exhausted.

The food was very poor, and inadequate, and this was always blamed on food shortages brought on by the War. For breakfast we had two spoonfuls of porridge sprinkled with salt, and one piece of bread and margarine. The porridge was almost always burnt, and we regularly had to pick cockroaches out of the bread. Dinner was usually a thin stew with lentils and a little onion, and one piece of bread.

The older girls cooked the meals in the kitchen which was situated in the boys' home and then brought across to our dining hall. Dinner was served from a huge bowl which stood on the floor in the corner of the room, and each week a different girl was given the task of ladling it out into the individual bowls. Once, when it was my turn, I was a few minutes late coming in from school, as I had been given a halfpenny by Mamma and had decided to buy some humbugs on the way back to the Home. Miss Tilly was furious, and when I knelt down to ladle out the first serving she pushed my head down into the big bowl, soaking my hair. Then she took away my sweets, which were a precious commodity in those wartime days.

When a girl left school at the age of fourteen she usually found herself working either in the kitchen or the laundry of the Home, perhaps not having the confidence to try her luck elsewhere — 'Better the devil you know'. A few girls stayed on until they were eighteen, and then they were placed in service.

We were able to attend our own school, where we were known as 'The Home Girls'. We wore a uniform which consisted of a blue twill dress, a striped calico petticoat and bloomers, and a rough calico chemise. We wore long black stockings, which, when washed, would turn green in patches, and black lace-up boots. Our outdoor coats were usually given to us by charitable organisations. Our stockings were always going into holes, and one night a week was given over to mending them and keeping all our clothes in good repair.

The older girls were detailed to inspect and fine-tooth comb the younger girls' hair, and woe betide anyone who was found to have nits — Miss Tilly would take a large pair of scissors, and with seemingly cruel delight would cut off the offending hair.

One of the hardest things to bear at the Home was the sight of between four and six girls standing outside Miss Martha's sitting-room daily, each one with a wet sheet on her head, having wet the bed the night before. They were waiting to be caned, and she would leave them standing outside her room for as long as she could, so that they became more and more fearful and totally humiliated.

Each night we would take turns at peeling the potatoes for the following day. This was done with the help of a barrel-like contraption out in the yard into which we would empty a sack of potatoes followed by several buckets of water, and turn the handle. It was very tiring work, but this duty was carried out in all weathers, hail, rain or snow, usually with empty potato sacks over our shoulders to help keep us warm.

Each Saturday there was extra work for me to do. The wooden stairs going from the dining room down to the locker room, where we spent what little free time we had, had to be scrubbed, and the area steps by which means we entered the house, had to be red-raddled.

On Saturday evenings we went to Church to the Confessional, and on Sunday mornings we went to Holy Communion. In those days it was customary to go to Church without so much as having a drink of water, and not being a strong child to begin with, I fainted in Church on regular occasions. I also fainted most mornings at school assembly, probably from hunger and strain.

If Mamma had time she came to meet us from school and walked us back to the Home — at least we had that privilege; and she was allowed to visit us one Sunday in each month.

Patsy stopped fretting after a while, which was a great help to me, but on one occasion whilst I was on 'potato duty' another girl found nits in Patsy's hair and reported it to Miss Tilly, who promptly cut every bit of it off. Another girl came to tell me about this, and I ran screaming to Miss Tilly demanding to know why she had cut all of my sister's lovely hair off, and saying I would have cleaned it myself. She slapped my face on both sides and told me to mind my own business and get on with the potatoes. I was heartbroken, both for myself and for poor Patsy.

There is one thing, however, that I do have to thank Miss Tilly for. She had a fair soprano voice, and when she was in a good mood she would call us into the dining room and teach us to sing rather lovely ballads. I had a good voice myself, possibly inherited from Mamma, and I loved those old songs. There was a piano there, but Miss Tilly couldn't play it and so we sang unaccompanied.

I was very like father in that I loved entertaining, and I arranged concerts at school which seemed to go down very well, and was often asked to sing solo.

The Committee gave us a party at Christmas-time. The first year I was at the Home I arranged to put on a pantomime, 'Cinderella'. We saved our meagre pocket-money and bought crepe paper to make dresses, and I taught the girls their parts, and how to dance and sing. The Committee decided the show was very good and worthwhile, and all the participants were given sixpence each for their efforts.

During the summer holidays from school we were all taken for a whole month to a resort called Moreton-on-the-Wirral, on the other side of the Mersey, which, generally speaking, made a very pleasant change from the Home, although Miss Tilly's constant presence tended to take the shine off what we looked upon as being a form of escape. There was certainly no escape from the hard work we were accustomed to, for the house we stayed at was very large and we had to scrub, polish and clean it. My job, as usual, was to clean down the stairs, which totally exhausted me. I scrubbed them daily with sand from the beach, which made them beautifully white, and quite impressed me. In fact, despite my exhaustion, when I had finished the task I would stand back to admire my handywork.

I remember one particular occasion during holiday time; we were sitting down to dinner when Mr Foster, the Manager of the Home called in to see us. What a sight met his eyes! We were all sitting around the table crying our eyes out because we found it impossible to eat the food placed before us, and Miss Tilly insisted that we did. She was punching us and slapping us, completely out of control until she became aware of Mr Foster's presence, which had an immediate calming effect on her. He ordered her to investigate what was wrong with the food, and it seemed that one of the kitchen girls had left a piece of soap on the side of the boiler in which the food was cooked, and it had slipped into the food, rendering it totally inedible. Mr Foster was very angry with Miss Tilly, and after giving her a good dressing down ordered her to arrange for some large tins of corned beef to be opened immediately, and sandwiches made for us all. A rare treat!

Mr Foster always came with us on these holidays, staying at a nearby hotel in a very pretty district called Upton.

On Sundays we all walked to Church. How I loved those walks — the hedgerows full of wild flowers and the smell of clover everywhere. At other times we would be taken down to the sea, and would swim from the embankment, part of which was being repaired by German prisoners of war who would enjoy watching our antics in the water. Miss Martha and Miss Tilly were keen swimmers and would consequently be in good humour, so that these occasions were high spots in our holiday.

All too soon we would be taken back to the Home, where life resumed its normal pattern.

I well remember an incident at the Home when a little boy, who was probably about three years old, came from the babies' home to stay in the girls' quarters. He was a little young to be transferred at all, and should really have gone into the boys' home when he left Nurse Lee. However, he was such a beautiful child, fair-haired and blue-eyed, and although he had obviously been rather spoiled, Miss Martha and Miss Tilly fell in love with him and kept him in our Home. His name was Frankie Vane.

Young Frankie was petted and fussed over, dressed very well, and never allowed to eat with us — always having his meals with Miss Martha and Miss Tilly. This state of affairs continued quite happily for some months until one of the girls, Rebecca, decided to investigate the difference between boys and girls in the dormitory one morning. Unfortunately Miss Tilly caught them, and poor Rebecca was severely caned, whilst little Frankie was banished to the boys' Home without any more ado.

I quite enjoyed going to school; not only to get away from the Home for a few hours each day, but also because I was very much involved with anything to do with the stage.

One year the teachers decided to arrange a concert in aid of the Soldiers and Sailors' Comforts Fund, and I was chosen to sing my solos. A small girl, whose name was Bella — also from the Home, and a real Shirley Temple type with a mop of red curls and a pretty little face, was chosen to sing and dance. She wore a very pretty white dress and a khaki cap, and she sang 'Take Me Back To Blighty'. The first night went well with her, but on the second night she forgot herself and parodied the words, singing 'Hey diddlee hytee, somebody stole me nightie and left me in me father's shirt'. This, of course, brought the house down, causing her to blush as only a redhead can. Poor Bella — she suffered with Petit Mal, and often would have a fit. On these occasions the teacher in charge, possibly through fear and ignorance, would shake Bella roughly for not paying attention.

The white dress that Bella wore for her performance was provided by the Home, and after the show it was taken back and put in a large chest of drawers on the landing outside my dormitory. One night, after lights-out, I decided to entertain the girls, so I struggled into the lovely white dress and was happily dancing, and singing quietly, when Miss Tilly came in and caught me. She gave me a few hard slaps and said: "Marie, I'll make you suffer for this". Nothing more was said about this affair until many months later, in the summer time when the day for the school picnic came along. We were to go to New Brighton, and Miss Tilly stood at the door counting us out. When it came to my turn she put her hand out and said: "You are not going anywhere Marie — you are going to be punished, and you know why". Then she set me to work, and in fact I worked for the whole of that day.

My first task was to light the fire which provided the hot water. There was an art to this; no-one liked having to do it, and needless to say I could not manage it at my first few attempts. Each time I failed to light it Miss Tilly would thump me on the back, and she carried on doing this until eventually I managed to succeed. After that I was made to scrub and polish throughout the whole building until around mid-afternoon, at which time I was told to get washed and go and help Elsie in the Pantry. Elsie was almost eighteen and had been instructed by Miss Tilly to look after the staff meals as part of her training for future hotel work in Liverpool.

What I saw in the Pantry astonished me. There was no lack of food there, even though every one of us girls suffered the pangs of hunger daily. Elsie was preparing afternoon tea for Miss Martha and Miss Tilly, and was setting the tray with plates of thinly-sliced bread spread thickly with butter. I was feeling very hungry, and the sight of this made my mouth water, so I asked her if I could have a piece. Not unkindly she said: "I dare not give it to you Marie; every single piece has been counted and I can't even have a piece myself". I was so upset, as the sight of the bread and butter reminded me of the days when father was alive and I wanted for nothing.

Memories of that particular day will always stay with me, and I will never understand how any woman could be so callous as to wait for months to punish a child for a small misdemeanor. I felt my heart was broken that day, but I would not allow Miss Tilly to break my spirit and tried to keep from her just how I felt.

Winter at the Home was hard for every one of the children there because nothing warm was provided for us to wear, and we wore the same clothes all the year round. Our poor hands were in a shocking state — especially mine which were always in water. When the snow covered the area steps I had to scrape it all off before I could red-raddle them, and my fingers were chapped and sore — wide open for infection to enter, which it did. Then, bread poultices were applied to my hands and they were bound around with dirty, wet bandages. I remember that I suffered greatly in this respect.

The War was going badly, and merchant ships were so often sunk in the Liverpool Bay that food rations were very hard to come by and we were hungry most of the time. Then came the terrible Influenza Epidemic. It laid us all low, and outside help had to brought in to nurse us. Some girls were transferred to the Babies' Home, putting added strain on Nurse Lee, and sadly, one girl in her care died. She was Lizzie, who was sister to Elsie who worked in the pantry. Elsie was confined to bed along with me and at least half of the other girls in my dormitory.

One night I became desperately ill and everyone expected me to die. I knew I was at death's door, and although in high fever I heard a midwife, who had volunteered to take over night-duty, say to Miss Tilly: "I doubt if this child will see the night through, but if she does survive this crisis then she'll be alright". Her words must have penetrated my subconcious and I willed myself to get better.

Tragedies were all around us during that terrible time and we heard of whole families being wiped out by this virulent infection. Our local newsagent lost his wife and all four of his children, leaving him alone and devastated. I was very fearful that Mamma would die and we might never be able to return to her.

Miss Tilly escaped this dreadful illness, and although Miss Martha was taken ill for a few days with the virus, she did not suffer as severely as most people — possibly because she was strong and well-fed.

When I was deemed to be better Miss Tilly made me get on with the cleaning, and once again delegated me to light that dreaded fire, despite the fact that I was still so weak I could hardly stand. Eventually I became stronger, but I can't remember ever feeling well the whole of the time spent at the Home.

One evening in the Spring we were at Church for Benediction and Mamma was there too. She took us aside and said: "I want you to meet a friend of mine". I thought nothing of it at the time and just shook hands politely with the man she introduced. He kissed me on the cheek, which I thought was rather strange, but I little realised the impact this man was going to make on our lives in the future.

When the War ended we were given a Victory Party by the Committee. Before the event I was taken, with another girl of around my age, to Mr Foster's office, which was off Dale Street in the city. He asked us in turn to read a poem; it was a Victory poem, and I was chosen to read it at the party. Mr Foster was very pleased with my rendering, and everything went well on the day.

Time went by, and eventually Mamma found a little house of her own. It was a small house — two up and two down in a quiet, respectable little street. Shortly before Patsy and I went home to our new house we were having a gramophone recital in the dining room when Miss Martha and Miss Tilly called us over to them and told us we would be going home soon as we had a new father. I was shattered; I never expected anything like this to happen.

Two weeks later new clothes arrived for us. I had a pink dress and Patsy had a brown one. Mamma then came for us, fulfilling the promise she had made to us so long ago, and a new chapter of our lives began.

Chapter VI

CHARLIE

On arrival at our new home I was delighted to see how very clean and neat it was, with even a few pieces of familiar furniture around, which gave me a feeling of belonging once more.

The house was in Godfrey Street — in a pleasant area of terraced houses. It was rather small, and from the front door we walked straight into the living room which boasted a coal fire and an oven. The fire was the only form of heating we had, which meant it had to be lit throughout the whole year to provide hot water for baths and domestic purposes, and also for cooking. Leading from the living room was a scullery with a stone sink and cold water tap, and from the scullery a flight of stairs led up to the two bedrooms. In the back yard was a lavatory, or 'Privvy' as it was then called, but 'we didn't have a garden, which initially disappointed me.

We were thrilled to be back with Mamma, and I happily set the table for tea which included home-made bread and butter, which to Patsy and me was sheer luxury. Undoubtedly, to me in particular, best butter represented a feeling of stability and security, and in my adult years I have never knowingly eaten margarine, deciding I would rather starve than engender the feelings of deprivation that the eating of margarine had once aroused in me.

Sadly, my feeling of jubilation was short-lived, because whilst we were eating our tea our new 'father' arrived home from work. The moment he entered the room I took a dislike to him, and in fact to my mind he brought with him such a strong sense of foreboding that I wanted to run away. His name was Charlie!

Mamma introduced him to us as our new father, and it was, we quickly realised, the same man she had introduced to us at Church a few months earlier. He was short in stature, his eyes were rather deep set, and his face was scarred, apparently the result of a number of operations he had had performed on him for reasons we were never able to determine.

On this first occasion Charlie had very little to say, but from that moment he had a huge impact on our lives.

Apparently Mamma had known Charlie when she was a young girl and she knew he came from a very wealthy and influential family in Liverpool and had received the best education possible until he was eighteen years of age. His brothers and sisters had all benefitted from their education and had done well in life, one sister becoming the head mistress of a well-known private school for girls, and two brothers who became lawyers. However, Charlie did not take after the rest of his family and quite simply did not like work.

Although Charlie was placed in a good position on leaving school, he never stayed in any one job for any length of time and his family despaired of him. In fact, he quickly became known as the black sheep of the family, and by the time he met up again with Mamma they had totally disowned him.

It seems their second meeting came about in a rather strange way through an old school friend of

Mamma's, Mary Perry, a widow with a young daughter, who lived in a very large house and who regularly took in lodgers, mostly of a theatrical leaning, and who were performing at one of the many popular and well-frequented theatres of the day; The Hippodrome, The Empire and the Olympia. She too had known Charlie in her younger days, and one day found him on her doorstep looking for accommodation. They talked about old times, and Mamma's name was mentioned. Mary herself did not have accommodation to offer at that particular time, but knowing where Mamma lived she sent him around to see her, suggesting that she might have a room to spare, and could most certainly do with the money.

At that time Patsy and I were still at the Home, and Mamma only had young George living with her, so despite her initial misgivings she gave in to his pleadings and let Charlie have a room.

When he first took up residence in Mamma's house Charlie had only the clothes he stood up in, and no luggage of any kind. However, he convinced her he had a good job lined up and would be starting work soon.

Being the character he was, Charlie knew that as soon as he got his foot over the doorstep he was on to a good thing, and so he lost no time in asking Mamma to marry him. She told me much later that she had desisted for quite a long time, but eventually he wore her down with his persuasions. In her heart of hearts she must have known what she was taking on, and Mamma of all people knew that a leopard does not change its spots. She was such a strong character that all of this was quite amazing, but nevertheless she bought him a new suit of clothes and married him in the local Catholic Church; Aunt Jane and Uncle Tom being the witnesses.

Around that time Mamma had a spate of good jobs going for her, because she was highly respected in the area and was recognised as a woman of character, clean habits, and determination. This made it even harder to understand why she had succumbed to Charlie's blandishments, and married him. I can only think she believed that after all our years of deprivation, we children needed a father to provide the stability we had so long been denied.

A number of midwives in the area recommended Mamma to well-off families where the wives needed nursing and caring for after a confinement. Always genteel of manner, she would totally fit the bill.

Before she married Charlie he had promised her she would never need to work again because he would work hard to provide for her and her three children. Needless to say, he had not changed character, and because of his idleness he continued to lose one job after another. In those days most people worked on Saturday mornings, but whilst Mamma would get up and go off to work at her usual week-day time, Charlie would regularly be lying in bed when she left, complaining of a headache, and would very often still be there when she returned home at lunchtime.

Mamma quickly realised that all she had done in marrying Charlie was to take on an extra burden, and her temper was awful to behold. Rows between her and Charlie were frequent and violent, and in comparison the altercations she had had with my father during his lifetime paled into insignificance.

Charlie's mother had died several years before he married Mamma, and his father lived alone in a big house in the Sefton Park area of Liverpool. One day, at the end of her tether, Mamma dressed my brother George nicely and took him to visit her new father-in-law. She rang the bell at the entrance to the big house and the door was opened by a maid to whom she introduced herself. The maid then went off to relay the news of his visitor to Charlie's father, who most certainly did not want to see Mamma, but because of her deep distress he eventually relented and asked her into the house. He told Mamma that Charlie's name was an anathema to him, and that even his wife, Charlie's mother, before she died had refused to visit Charlie when he was once in hospital and thought to be on his death bed. However, Mamma pleaded with him to use his influence in helping to get Charlie a job, and eventually he agreed to help, despite the fact that he was of the opinion that Mamma must have known what she was taking on when she married him.

As a result of this visit Charlie was offered a job as a night-watchman on a building site for the Liverpool Corporation, and although the job did not pay well it suited him down to the ground, keeping him warm and comfortable at night, with no-one breathing down his neck to make sure he worked. This meant that Mamma worked during the day and Charlie worked at night time, so that the rows between them were less frequent and we were all able to breathe a little more easily.

Chapter VII

INDEPENDENCE

On the bright side, we children renewed our acquaintanceship with our cousins, Dolly, Bunty and Fred. They knew Liverpool very well, of course, and we would be allowed to join them on excursions into town. I quickly learned that not everyone in Liverpool was a drunken Hooligan. To my surprise and delight I came across some spotlessly clean homes where I least expected to find them, and I discovered that most Liverpudlians are amongst the kindest people in the whole wide world.

I loved going to the landing stage at the Pier Head and watching the big liners come and go. They were the Queens of the Seas, coming from America, 'Hobart, Quebec and Vancouver'. I was fascinated by the overhead railway, St. George's Hall with its lovely gardens, and the Liverpool Museum, with all those steps to climb. What treasures they held for all to see. When I discovered the Walker Art Gallery I was overcome with joy.

Another place I loved was Lime Street Station with the old steam trains puffing in like monsters, seemingly from other worlds. I remember that the rail fare to Birmingham was five shillings, and I badly wanted Mamma to be able to afford to take a trip back there. Sadly she never had the money to spare for such a luxury — five shillings was a lot of money in those days.

I was coming up to twelve years of age when I had the first stirrings of independence, and I felt the need to have some money of my own. So I found myself a little job in a baker's shop which paid me two shillings and sixpence a week, and for which I had to work for one hour during my school lunch break, from Monday to Thursday, and a half day on Saturday. I had to deliver bread on a truck so heavy that I honestly don't know how I managed to push it, especially since most of my journey was uphill. The truck was made of very thick planks of wood, with cast-iron wheels and two long wooden handles. I delivered bread to private houses as well as to a number of shops in the area.

The truck would be loaded and waiting for me at lunch-time each day, and after I had delivered the bread I would dash home for a bite of lunch and a quick wash, and then dash back to school. Patsy would be home at lunch-time well before me, and since she had a very healthy appetite, I would very often find there was nothing nourishing for me to eat and would make do with a few slices of bread and butter.

Mamma was still finding it difficult to make ends meet, and so I would give her over half my weekly wages, and after work on Saturday mornings the manageress of the shop would often give me half a dozen cakes to take home with me, which also helped out.

Unfortunately, however, the hard work soon took its toll of my health, and many times Mamma would come home at tea-time to find me lying on the bed, totally exhausted, and with a bad headache. I continued to struggle on, despite the fact that I was losing weight, having night sweats and losing my appetite. Mamma began to seriously worry about me and took me once more to the doctor, only to be given the same advice as all those years ago — "a bottle of stout each night, and get her hair cut".

Came the summer, and the school holidays, and those children who could afford to were going off to Rhyl in North Wales, for two weeks holiday by the sea. Somehow or another Mamma managed to raise the money, and I went along with them. Whilst I was there I felt so very much better, and really enjoyed the change, so that on my return Mamma was delighted to see me looking so well again, but sadly, only for a short while.

It became more and more difficult to push that heavy truck full of bread, and in fact it was becoming almost impossible for me to walk upright. I also developed severe pains between my shoulders, and Mamma took the advice of a friend who recommended a different doctor. When we reached the doctor's surgery he took one look at me and said to Mamma: "Take this child home and put her to bed, and I will come and examine her first thing tomorrow morning". He was as good as his word, and after he had examined me he said I had Tuberculosis and must go to hospital immediately.

I was admitted to Alder Hey Hospital in Liverpool, one of the finest children's hospitals in the country to this very day, where I spent the happiest twelve months of my early years.

Chapter VIII

ALDER HEY HOSPITAL

In those days the only treatment for Tuberculosis was fresh air, plenty of rest and good food, and I had all three in abundance at Alder Hey Hospital — sleeping day and night on a secluded balcony, having much needed rest, and being offered a choice of all types of delectable food.

I was twelve years old and was placed in a ward with girls of different ages, all of whom became my friends. Sadly, some of them died, sometimes overnight — almost without warning — being there one day and gone the next, filling me with great sadness.

I was lucky and started to get better quickly, and I thoroughly enjoyed being spoiled by the lovely nurses who used to brush my long hair and vie with each other as to who would buy the best ribbons to adorn it. I had only to wish for something and it was mine, especially books, which I had always loved. Gradually I was allowed out of bed for short spells, and Mamma, Patsy, George and Charlie were given permission to visit me every fourth Sunday.

Children with T.B. bones were allowed to go to the school-room each day as they were considered to have a 'closed' infection, but in my ward schooling was taboo.

During the summer months a Police Band regularly came to play on the hospital lawns and children who were not confined to bed were taken out to listen. One Sunday morning it rained heavily, but the sun came out in the afternoon and the Band turned up as usual. I was happily listening to the music when I happened to glance down, and to my horror saw a big fat worm beside my chair. I put my feet up on the rungs of the chair and closed my eyes. When I next looked down the lawn was carpeted with worms so I stood on the chair and screamed. Obviously the rain had brought them to the surface, and the boys that were around started to pick them up and throw them at the girls. I can remember one hitting me on the side of my neck and I promptly fainted, in consequence of which the Band broke up in confusion.

I was really sorry about that incident, but I have always been terrified of worms and have never been able to overcome those fears despite my love of gardening.

The hospital had catered entirely for wounded soldiers during the War, but those not fit enough to go home had remained and were accommodated in Nissen huts in the grounds. One of these soldiers was a Captain Lipscombe, who hailed from Kent, and he had a tubercular infection in a wound in his arm. He was very sweet on one of our nurses, Nurse Lewis, and I'm sure she cared for him too.

In those days hospital wards were heated by coal fires and we had lovely times sitting around them, laughing, talking, and playing guessing games. Captain Lipscombe was always present if his pretty little nurse was on duty, and on one particular occasion the subject of marriage came up. Captain Lipscombe smiled at Nurse Lewis, who smiled back fondly at him, and although I had no reason to say it, and I don't know where the premonition came from,

I turned to her and said: "Nurse Lewis, you will never be married". She laughed at me and said: "Why do you say that Marie?" Of course I could not explain, but a few short weeks later she died of peritonitis. Undoubtedly this was my first psychic experience.

Alder Hey Hospital, Eaton Road

We all missed Nurse Lewis greatly, and I personally have her to thank for one of the greatest experiences of my life. She obtained permission to take me to the theatre, where we had a box, and I witnessed a fantastic performance of the great Pavlova in "Swan Lake". I'll always remember her with deep affection.

The nurses on our ward always gave a tea party for patients on the occasion of their birthdays, and I would be only too happy to arrange a concert. My cousin Dolly would come along to play the piano, and I would sing — although at that time I found singing rather difficult because my breathing was affected by my tubercular condition. Nevertheless, everyone seemed to be delighted by my voice as I rendered the ballads Miss Tilly had taught me.

After these concerts Captain Lipscombe would present us with flowers, and I can remember feeling so proud; in my girlish imagination I felt I could easily become a film star, or perhaps a famous ballerina. Then again, I might settle for being a poet or an authoress, although I had no idea how I would ever achieve any of these things.

Eventually Captain Lipscombe recovered sufficiently to be sent home, and I cried for him unashamedly. I corresponded with him for a few years, and will never forget his many kindnesses to all of us.

A short while before I was discharged a beautiful Indian girl was admitted to my ward. She was very ill indeed, and for some reason she never ever lay down. She always sat with her legs crossed, and looked at us with large, sad eyes. She was fourteen years old and could not speak any English at all. Her name was Mahendra.

One night Mahendra passed away in her sleep and the Salvation Army people came to lay her out on her mother's instructions. The following day I was helping one of the nurses to change the linen on the beds and was asked to go along to the linen room to collect some clean sheets. On entering the room I saw that Mahendra had been laid out on one of the shelves, awaiting the mortuary attendants. At last she was lying down, but her poor legs were fixed in the cross-legged position in which she had died. Her long hair was plaited and tied with white satin ribbon; she wore a blue dress, a white satin underslip and white stockings. On her forehead was a jewelled headband and her arms were embellished with gold bracelets. She looked so beautiful that I stood and gazed at her for a little while, quite unafraid; having by this time become quite matter of fact about death. When I returned to the nurse, handing her the clean sheets I asked her: "Whatever will they do with Mahendra's legs?" "Oh", she replied "They'll have to break them". Only then did I weep for Mahendra.

I continued to make good progress, and eventually the day came for me to be discharged from the hospital. Mamma came to collect me, and I can well remember the doctor saying to her: "Of course, Marie is very much better, but you must realise there is no cure for Tuberculosis and she will have to be well looked after for the rest of her days". How very true his words were, for the Tuberculosis lingered in my body, and in my middle years it almost took my life.

Chapter IX

BACK TO SCHOOL

On returning home from the hospital I had a short break and then commenced my schooling. I was then thirteen years old and had missed twelve months education and was due to leave school when I was fourteen. I tried very hard to catch up with the other girls, but I doubt if I did.

At school I had a very good friend, Josie. In fact we are still friends to this day, and although she has lived in America for most of her adult life we still keep in touch.

Josie brought me up to date as to what had been happening at school in my absence, and of particular interest to me was the fact that they had been taking cookery and laundry lessons. I would have loved to have been there on the day when the girls had been making bread in class, and were coming out of school, each of them carrying a lovely warm loaf, when they met the school inspector going in. The inspector stopped, and asked them one or two questions about their cookery lessons, and eventually asked them what they enjoyed baking most of all. Julie, another of Josie's friends, immediately spoke up, saying: "Oh, we like making bread Miss", and when the inspector asked her:"Why", Julie said: "Because it makes our hands so lovely and clean Miss". This incident was reported to one of the teachers, Sister Mary Winifred, who was very well-liked, and was, in fact, my favourite. She was apparently very angry indeed and made sure that the Cookery Class was kept in after school-hours to learn all about hygiene.

My sister, Patsy, behaved very badly at school, never paying attention and consequently not learning very much. One day Sister Mary Winifred sent for me to ask if I could use my influence to get Patsy to desist from using a sharp instrument to carve outlines of naked ladies on her desk lid. I really liked this particular teacher, who always seemed fair, and I would have done whatever I could to please her. However, in the case of Patsy it was impossible; by this time she was a strapping, well-made girl, with a mind of her own, and I no longer had any influence over her.

My friend Josie and I often visited each other in the evenings after school, but as Mamma would never allow any of our friends into the house we had to talk to them on the doorstep when they called. I always felt this was because Mamma did not really want to share us with anyone else, having been separated from us for so long.

One day I went to visit Josie at her home, and although she usually invited me inside, on this occasion she kept me on the doorstep, saying I had better not go in because her mother had been confined that day. I had no idea what this meant, and on asking Josie she told me that her mother had just given birth to a baby girl and they were calling her Marie.

I was so innocent that I never had any curiosity at all as to where babies came from, and I never thought to ask.

Josie already had one brother, who was in hospital with Tuberculosis, and a sister of school age. Sadly, her brother eventually died of this dreadful disease, and Josie herself had to have a T.B. gland removed from her neck, leaving a nasty scar.

In those days Tuberculosis was called the English disease — thank God we now have a cure for it.

The following Easter I was fouteen years old and my school mistress asked me to bring in a copy of my birth certificate, to prove my age. When I asked Mamma for this she said: "Oh, I've mislaid it — I'll send for your baptismal certificate which will only cost six pence". I knew that a copy birth certificate also cost only six pence, but I didn't query the matter and my teacher was quite happy to accept my baptismal certificate as proof of my age.

Mamma always tried to buy something new for us to wear at Easter time, and this particular year she bought Patsy and me new brown coats and matching brown shoes, fancy straw hats trimmed with velvet ribbons and cream coloured flowers. She said we could wear our outfits to Church on Sunday, weather permitting, and although the day dawned with light drizzle, it eventually stopped for a while, so Patsy and I prevailed upon Mamma to let us dress up in all our glory.

We arrived at Church feeling very grand, but as we were not permitted to either eat or drink before attending Communion we sometimes felt rather faint, and on this occasion Patsy chose to have a fainting attack about halfway through the service. I somehow managed to drag her to the side door for fresh air, which I badly needed myself by this time. No one came to help us but I managed to pull the heavy door open intending to sit Patsy down on the Church steps, but of course she fell, dragging me down with her. While we had been inside the Church it had rained heavily, and we both rolled down about ten muddy steps; our new hats came off and our new coats were covered in mud, and when we eventually arrived back home we were in a very sorry state.

At the sight of us Mamma was absolutely speechless; it must have been a bitter blow after all the expense she had gone to in providing our new outfits. Fortunately, after they were cleaned, we were able to wear them again.

In the summer of that year I left school, and with great excitement, and not a little trepidation, I set out to find myself a job in the big wide world.

Chapter X

MY FIRST JOB

I had no idea what I wanted to do with the rest of my life, but Mamma suggested I should try for an apprenticeship with one of the top milliners in town. To please her I allowed myself to be taken along for an interview, which seemed to go well, but after that I had to take a sewing test, and although I kept it to myself I was delighted when they told me I had not passed, because I had always hated sewing of any kind, and in fact I still do.

Eventually I found myself a position as a cashier in one of the larger stores in Liverpool — Blacklers — in the Fur and Flowers department on the ground floor. I had to wear a navy blue dress with a white collar, and I must confess that this outfit quite went to my head and I thought I was the belle of the ball.

I really enjoyed my job, and did so well that quite soon I was promoted to the Gent's Tailoring Department, which was staffed entirely by men, apart from myself. I felt a little embarrassed in these new surroundings, unlike the young girl who took over from me at lunch time, who absolutely loved it. Her name was Polly, and she really was a forward young lady who was forever cheeking the male members of the staff. For the most part they didn't seem to mind too much.

One day Polly asked me if I had a spare sanitary towel, and when I asked her what kind of a towel was that she said: "You really mean you don't know?" I shook my head and she suggested I should have a talk with my mother that evening. Unfortunately I didn't bring the subject up with Mamma, and so I suffered the consequences when my periods started. Having seen so many haemmorrhages when I was in hospital I thought I was ill again when my first period arrived, and so I tried to keep it to myself, but Mamma found out when I soiled the bed-sheet and responded merely by handing me a packet of sanitary towels, with no explanation whatsoever. I was really miserable and confused, and eventually begged Polly to explain it all to me.

My next promotion at work was to the Stationery Department down in the basement, which was rather airless and stuffy. Consequently I fainted regularly, which must have been very inconvenient for everyone concerned. Despite this I was happy in my job, which was well-paid for those days. I earned seven shillings and six pence a week and dinner and tea was provided for all the staff on Fridays and Saturdays. The hours were long and I worked until seven o'clock at night on Thursdays, eight o'clock on Fridays and nine o'clock on Saturdays, although we did have Wednesday afternoon free. Out of my wages I gave Mamma six shillings and six pence and with the shilling left over I paid six pence on the tram journeys home, two pence for a magazine called Peg's Paper, which I had to hide from Mamma because she did not consider it suitable reading for a young lady, two pence for a chocolate cream whirl, and two pence for the Liverpool Weekly Post, which Mamma loved to read.

During this period of my life Mamma would warn me to keep away from boys, which I did not understand and she never explained. On one occasion my friend Josie called, and whispered to me that she had a blind date fixed up for both of us and we would be going to the cinema the following day. I agreed to go, not knowing what it all meant, and I merely told Mamma I was going out with Josie. She gave me strict instructions to be home by nine o'clock, and her parting shot to me was: "I'll know if you've been with any boys".

When I met Josie outside the cinema I discovered that our blind date was two young soldiers. Josie introduced me to them and we all went inside, where to my dismay I was separated from Josie and her soldier, and had to sit further back from them with my date. Remembering the incident with the soldiers in the park when I was a child, I was quite petrified when the young soldier reached for my hand and held it tightly. Not a word passed between us, and when he eventually excused himself to go to the toilet I arose quietly and fled the place as if all the devils in Hell were after me.

I was very subdued for a few days, feeling sure Mamma would find out what I had been up to. She never did, but Josie was not at all pleased with me, saying she imagined I had been kidnapped.

The summer of that year was unusually hot and the basement of the store in which I worked became unbearably stuffy; so much so that on one particular Saturday afternoon I fainted several times, causing acute consternation amongst the staff and customers alike. In consequence of this the management felt they had no alternative but to ask me to leave.

I hated having to tell Mamma this, and kept the news from her until the following Monday morning, but when I did tell her she appeared to be rather relieved, as she felt my health was beginning to fail again and she preferred me to be with her.

Shortly after I lost my job Mamma saw an advertisement in the Liverpool Echo asking for a husband, wife and daughter team to manage a Sweets and Tobacconist shop which also sold soft drinks and herbal remedies. She applied for the job and was accepted, possibly because of her previous shop experience and her excellent references. I pleaded with her to turn the offer down, mainly because the shop was situated in one of the most depressed areas of Liverpool and I couldn't bear the thought of leaving our lovely little house in Godfrey Street. However, she was adamant, saying that this time, if we all pulled together, we could make a success of it.

Patsy and George were as unhappy as I was about moving, but once Mamma had made her mind up there was no changing it.

Chapter XI

THE SHOP

The shop was in Great Homer Street in what was fondly known as a 'Court' which consisted of six delapidated houses and shops on two sides and four running across the top. It was so very noisy in comparison with the quiet little backwater we had just left.

Heavy draught horses pulled their loads of corn up and down the street, seemingly all day long, and at least once a day a drover would drive cattle along the middle of the road to the cattle market which was at the end of the Court.

Mamma's fear of cows didn't help very much, because as soon as she espied the cattle approaching from some distance away she would gather us all up and run with us down a side street into a narrow passageway, which we called 'the jigger', and there we would stand in fear and trembling until she was certain that every last animal had passed by.

The living quarters were the worst we had ever encountered. The bedrooms were verminous, and Patsy, George and I kept well away from them until after Mamma had had them fumigated.

Eventually, between us, we managed to get the place clean and smartened up, and I remember we were not the only people in the Court who took a certain pride in their home; one or two of our neighbours boasted white door steps and clean curtains, and one neighbour's window-sill boasted a geranium plant. We were amazed at its ability to bloom in such a dark and dismal atmosphere — it was almost like an oasis in the desert.

Charlie still kept his job as night watchman for the Liverpool Corporation, and his job in the shop mainly concerned tapping the barrels of Sarsparilla and Ginger Ale in the cellar, and making Soda Water, whilst Mamma and I ran the shop between us.

The hours of opening were from nine o'clock in the morning until eleven o'clock at night, and our combined wage was a mere thirty shillings per week plus six pence in the pound commission and rent-free accommodation.

The War was over, and poverty hung all around us. The sight of ex-servicemen openly begging, or singing in the street for a few coppers was heart-breaking.

One poor young man used to come to our area every Thursday to beg. He had only one leg, but he always looked very clean and smart, and with his excellent baritone voice he would sing songs such as 'Avalon" and "Amazon River of Dreams". Poor fellow, his dreams must have been shattered long since!

Very few babies born in that area survived for any length of time — malnutrition and the conditions in which they lived took their toll, and funerals were regular occurrences.

The shop-keepers in our street lost no time in telling us that no-one ever stayed very long in our particular premises as it had the reputation of being haunted. This did not cause Mamma any great alarm because she was a firm believer in spiritualism and the supernatural. For myself, I just could not imagine how she was ever going to make a success of a business which sold what were virtual luxuries in those days, such as ice-cream and soft drinks, when everyone around us could barely afford the bare necessities of life.

Once we had settled in I decided I quite liked being behind the counter, and since Mamma was a great talker she attracted people back to the shop regularly to listen to her tales. However, I didn't like the long hours we were forced to work — we dare not close one second before eleven at night because the son of the owner of the shop regularly appeared on the corner of the street — sent by his father to make sure we didn't close before the appointed time.

Patsy and George were still attending school when we first moved in, so they had no involvement with the shop, but Mamma thought she would give Charlie a chance to prove himself behind the counter and gave him a trial period. This did not work out at all because, apart from helping himself to cigarettes, reducing our meagre profits, he would just not put himself out to be pleasant to the customers as Mamma and I did.

Charlie also became madly jealous of Mamma if she so much as spoke to a male customer, and rows between them became frequent.

There was a little window cunningly concealed between the shop and the living room where we could sit when there were no customers in the shop, and from which vantage point we could see when anyone came in. Charlie started sitting by this window watching Mamma's every move, and it must have been quite nerve-racking for her. He regularly refused to go down to the cellar to tap the barrels of ginger ale and to make soda water, and then the onus to do these jobs was put on Mamma and me.

I was shocked to discover that most of our male customers were meths. drinkers, who would come into the shop once the public houses had closed in the afternoon and buy soft drinks to mix with the meths. and disguise its bitter taste. These men were invariably amongst the more affluent people in the area, being corn merchants, money lenders, or successful shop-keepers, which was even more surprising.

The manageress of the local draper's shop was a pleasant middle-aged lady called Deborah Wyvel, and she and Mamma became good friends. We Christened her 'Dancing Deborah' because her main joy in life was dancing, and she regularly frequented the local dance halls. She had a daughter, May, who was about my age, and after some persuasion Mamma allowed me to go with May to dancing classes, which was the beginning of a social life for me.

I was coming up to sixteen years of age and took to dancing like a duck to water, so that very soon I became competent enough to venture into the dance halls. We knew a little 'sewing lady' who was a customer of ours, and she would sometimes make me a pretty little blouse or dance dress for just a few coppers. How she did it I don't know, but I was very grateful to her because I was bidding to be a real 'flapper' of the time, and to this end went out one day and had my waist-length hair 'bobbed'. Mamma was so angry with me for having this done that she refused to let me go out of the house for a whole week, and when I was eventually allowed out she would call after me: "Don't go near boys".

Since leaving school I had kept in touch with my very good friend, Josie, and sometimes she would accompany me to a dance hall, but mostly I was chaperoned by 'Dancing Deborah' and her daughter. Now and then a boy would ask to see me home, but I was never able to allow this, being so afraid that Mamma would find out and stop me from going out at all.

Financially it was very difficult to make ends meet. We seldom took more than twenty-five pounds weekly, which provided us with a wage of around thirty shillings, and despite the fact that Charlie was still continuing his night watchman job it was hardly enough to feed and clothe five people, and I was terrified Mamma would start to use the money lenders.

Just before Christmas at the shop, Charlie borrowed five pounds from a very kind customer, claiming it was to help Mamma to get by over the Christmas period. Of course it wasn't for that reason at all, and Charlie disappeared with the money without a word to us, and it was quite a long time before he came back into our lives.

In the meantime Mamma had to pay the customer the five pounds back, so once again we were back on the breadline, this time with a vengeance. To compensate for this, living without Charlie was like living in Paradise — no more spying, no more rows — it was blissful, despite the hardships.

When the shop was empty of customers Mamma and I would often sit down together, undisturbed, and she would relate to me the tales of her own youth, telling me that her parents were both alcoholics and almost always drunk. However, they would sober up a little on Friday evenings before going to Confession, but as soon as they left the Church they would head straight for the local public house to make up for lost time. All three of their daughters left home as soon as they could escape, and vowed never to see their parents again.

I did meet my maternal grandmother on one occasion only, shortly after my grandfather died — no doubt of alcoholic poisoning, and she did her best to drag Mamma and me into the nearest public house, saying I looked as if I was in need of a Guiness.

Mamma never told me I was born out of wedlock, and as if to appease some imagined feelings of guilt she would sometimes romance about her wedding, telling me she was married to my father in our local Catholic Church, in white, with Aunt Jane as her Matron of Honour, and riding in an open carriage. Had she told me the truth I would have loved her none the less. I can only imagine that she and father were married in a registry office, because in my later years I searched the Church register for a record of their marriage, in vain.

When Christmas Day arrived we were inundated by small children in the shop all day long, buying hot drinks and ice-cream with the few pennies they had been given as a Christmas treat. Normally we charged two pence for hot drinks, but because it was Christmas we charged just one penny.

Most of the children were dressed reasonably well on that day, and none of them was barefoot. It seems that the Liverpool Police Force had provided warm boots for under-privileged children, and the boots were marked in such a way that the pawnbrokers were not able to pledge them.

We didn't really have enough time to celebrate Christmas Day ourselves, as a family, business having to come first, but Patsy and George came in and out of the shop, enjoying the atmosphere created by the excitement of our young customers, and when we reckoned up our takings at the end of the day we found we had the best turnover ever.

After Christmas, Patsy, who was by this time fourteen, started work at the local Dunlop factory, which certainly helped the family budget along a little, and we were all feeling reasonably pleased with ourselves.

We had almost forgotten Charlie, but one day towards the end of the winter, when the snow was on the ground, Mamma had a glimpse of him standing on the corner of our road. The first time she ignored him and came hurrying home, but he started to appear there regularly looking cold and forlorn, and eventually she weakened and went to talk to him. He asked if he could come home, and although Patsy, George and I pleaded with her not to have him back she was too soft-hearted, and back he came. He was very quiet and well-behaved for a little while, and then the usual stormy scenes began all over again.

Shortly after Charlie's return our ghost surfaced. We were sitting around the table having supper one evening when a vase, which stood on an old dresser alongside of the open staircase, suddenly rose into the air and crashed to the floor, without breaking.

The only way the vase could have been reached would have been by someone putting a hand through the bannister, and there was no-one in that area. We all stared in utter amazement, but we were more puzzled than upset, and Mamma made very light of it.

. This same incident happened on a number of occasions until we came to accept it almost as a normal occurrence, but Mamma did eventually tire of it saying that sooner or later the vase would get broken, and as she was particularly fond of it she didn't want that to happen. So it was put away safely in a drawer.

A week or two later, during the evening, Mamma went into the shop to serve a customer, leaving me sitting in a rocking chair near the bottom of the stairs, reading a book. A sudden movement made me look up towards the stairs, and to my surprise I saw a child of about two years old coming down the staircase towards me — a pretty little girl with blonde hair and a mischevious face and wearing a long white nightdress. She put her little face between the bannisters and smiled at me, and then calmly continued walking down the stairs and straight through the closed door at the bottom.

Almost immediately Mamma came in from the shop, through the same door as the little girl had disappeared, and I very excitedly said: "Mamma, did you see her — the little blonde girl— she came down the stairs and walked straight through the door, without opening it". "I didn't see her" replied Mamma, "you must have been dreaming". But I knew I hadn't been dreaming, and something in the tone of Mamma's voice told me she was quite aware of the 'presence' of the child around the house but didn't want to alarm me by admitting it. In later years she did, in fact, confirm my suspicions.

Shortly after this incident Mamma did have cause to feel nervous. She was about to descend the stairs one morning and had just placed her foot on the first step, when without stumbling and without warning of any kind she fell from top to bottom. She swore some unseen hand had pushed her in the middle of her back, and despite her belief in the supernatural this was certainly not what she expected of it. Fortunately no bones were broken, but she was quite badly bruised and suffered a good deal of pain for some considerable time afterwards.

Some years later, after we had left the shop, we learned that the new tenant, who was a sensible and mature lady, stayed no longer than two weeks because an unseen presence on the stairs was trying to incite her to hang herself.

I was growing up fast, and was eventually considered to be a blossoming young lady by the male shop-keepers, who started to whistle after me in the street, causing me to blush to the roots of my hair. But I was still very innocent.

I remember one Sunday lunchtime when I idly picked up a copy of the News of The World from the counter in the shop and sat myself down to read it in the usual spot by the concealed window. The headline of the newspaper shrieked 'Fatty Arbuckle rapes Virginia Rapp'. I studied this for a moment and then casually called into the living room: "Mamma, what does rape mean?" Her reaction was immediate.

She grabbed the newspaper from me, boxed my ears, and told me never to read such a newspaper again. This was all very confusing to an adolescent girl — 'don't read newspapers — keep away from boys' but never an explanation as to "Why?"

My brother George was growing up rapidly into a very handsome young man. Mamma had the idea she would like him to be a priest when he was old enough. George, however, had other ideas and told her he was going to see the world when he was old enough, and the only way he could do this was by becoming a merchant seaman and going to sea.

In the meantime he set his heart on having a dog, and would encourage any stray dog to follow him home from school where he would feed it with bits and pieces of his dinner on the doorstep. This was a regular happening, but Mamma would not yield, even for George, although she did eventually buy him a rabbit, which pacified him for a while.

When George left school at fourteen one of his friends got him a job on one of the big liners. Mamma broke her heart about him going away, but he had to do something with his young life, and away he went to become a seaman. Whenever his ship docked at Liverpool he would come home to visit us, which created much excitement, and Mamma would always be there at the dock when his ship came in and we would all be eager and thrilled to hear of his exploits in foreign parts.

Shortly after George left home to become a seaman Mamma developed what she considered to be severe bouts of indigestion, which gave her a good deal of pain and caused her to lose weight. She was

very stoic about this, seldom complaining, although
she couldn't really hide it from me. Thankfully she
would, from time to time, put some weight back on
and enjoy some respite from the pain. With my help
she continued running the shop, and we did our very
best to earn a reasonable living from it.

"Aquitania" *in Gladstone Dock, May 1914*

Chapter XII

ROBERT

I continued my regular nights out at the local dance hall and became more and more proficient at learning the latest steps. These occasions were the highlights of my life, and after a while Mamma relaxed a little and did not always insist on me being chaperoned.

One evening I decided to branch out further afield and bravely took myself off to a dance hall in another district which had the reputation of attracting a nice type of person, and some really good dancers.

The dancing was in full swing when I arrived and I was soon enjoying myself and showing off my style. During an excuse-me waltz I danced briefly with 'every girl's dream' — a tall, dark and very handsome young man who set my heart beating rapidly the moment he took me in his arms. Later that evening I noticed him watching me, and when he realised I was not with a regular partner he asked me to dance again, and never left my side for the rest of the evening. His name was Robert.

At the end of the evening my dream boy asked if he could take me home, and I readily agreed, although I didn't let him venture any further than the bottom of our road in case Mamma saw me with him.

Robert didn't even try to kiss me, but he did ask if I would go out with him the following Sunday, and despite my fear of Mamma's reaction I readily agreed. Much to my surprise, when I told Mamma I had made a date to go out with a nice young man, she

Marie aged 18

Robert aged 20

Robert and Marie were engaged on 2nd August, 1924 and married on 3rd March. 1925

didn't demur, apart from saying: "Mind you behave yourself".

I was in a turmoil until Sunday came, never believing Robert would turn up, but at the appointed time there he was, and my heart raced as I walked shyly towards him.

Even though I had never been out with a boy before, and young as I was, I knew that this young man was going to play a very important role in my life and would be very special to me.

Robert told me he was apprenticed to an engineering company, and in his spare time he ran a little school of dancing to earn some extra money. He told me how much he admired my dancing style and asked if I would partner him in teaching the latest dances. I felt so very grown-up, and I happily agreed.

It all seemed like a fairy tale to me. I was only seventeen — I was the princess and Robert was my Prince Charming.

We started courting seriously almost from that first date, and eventually I invited him home to meet Mamma, with my heart in my mouth. She greeted him in a friendly way, and I could see she was immediately impressed with both his manner and appearance. However, she became distinctly cool when enquiring as to Robert's religion he told her, quite proudly, that he was a Protestant.

After Robert had gone home Mamma rounded on me and said I had better forget him, because nice though he seemed to be, there was absolutely no question of my marrying anyone who was not a Catholic. I didn't fuss too much about this because I knew in my heart that whatever obstacles were put in our path, Robert and I would be married one day.

When he took me home to meet his family the first thing his mother asked me, almost as soon as I got through the door, was: "And what religion are you?", to which I replied: "I'm Catholic". She made no attempt to hide her feelings in the matter, telling us that our relationship must end, at once, as otherwise Robert would be disowned. I was upset and embarrassed, but Robert took it all in his stride, and after introducing me to his father we quietly left — his mother looking like thunder and his father looking as though he didn't want any part of it.

Robert had three brothers and three sisters, and they were all, to one degree or another, under their mother's domination, and their father did not appear to play a very big part in their lives.

Despite the opposition, Robert and I were determined that nothing on earth would keep us apart. We were in love, and young as we were we wanted to get married as soon as possible to save any further upsets — even at one time considering eloping. However, I could not have left Mamma at that stage because her periods of ill-health were becoming more and more regular and acute. In fact, I feel it was because of her ill-health that she eventually weakened, recognising that Robert was a hardworking and reliable young man who would be a steadying influence on Patsy and George if anything happened to her.

So Robert and I were quietly married in a register office, and afterwards spent a blissful week on honeymoon in North Wales. Because we knew

Robert's mother would have made terrible scenes had she known about our wedding plans, his family were not informed of our marriage until we returned from honeymoon, and I believe her wrath was awful to behold when she heard the news. But nothing could mar our joy; we just knew we were meant for each other, and had plans to live "happily ever after".

Robert moved in with us until I became pregnant, and then we gave up the shop and moved into a large, comfortable house in a pleasant area on the outskirts of the city.

When our first daughter was born we called her Joy, because we were so happy, and although other daughters were born to us, each of them beautiful, we honestly believed there was no lovelier baby in the world than our little Joy.

Robert and I remained in love until the day he died at the age of 77, and I can honestly say that despite life's natural hardships I had butter on my bread from the moment we met.

Robert and Marie 1947

Epilogue

Patsy and George both married and raised families, and in particular George made a very happy marriage once he had got the sea out of his system, and he and his wife, Alice, raised two lovely daughters.

My cousin Dolly became a school teacher, and her sister Bunty married a handsome Naval Officer and went off to live in America. Cousin Fred married a beautiful girl who bore him four children, but sadly he died whilst still a young man. Cousin Tony, who we first met when sitting in his high chair, became a priest, at Uncle Tom's insistence.

Mamma lived on to see, and to help me raise my daughters, battling on until 1935 before the cancer which was causing her 'indigestion' took her life. On her deathbed she asked me if I would take care of Charlie, and albeit reluctantly I said I would.

Charlie married again, no more successfully than his marriage to Mamma. He would regularly leave his wife, and after a period of roaming appear on the corner of the road we lived in. On their way home from school my daughters would see him standing there, and would drag him home with them so excitedly that I couldn't turn him away. He was the only grandfather they knew, and they adored him, and I have to say that he was devoted to them. After I had fed and re-clothed him Charlie would stay with us for a few weeks and then suddenly disappear, leaving my little daughters bewildered and upset. This pattern of behaviour continued throughout his life, and when eventually news came through from his second wife that he had died in hospital — about ten years after Mamma's death, my daughters wept bitterly.

It took me a long time to come to terms with Mamma's death and I missed her dreadfully. Often I would feel she was still around, and I certainly felt her presence strongly one evening when I was pregnant with my last daughter. I was sitting by the bedside, idly rubbing oil into my breasts — having been told this would help to prevent stretch marks, when to my horror I felt a small, hard lump in the left one. Instinctively I called out: "Oh, Mamma" and then I promptly fainted.

When I came to, Robert was comforting me and asking me what was wrong, and when I showed him the lump he passified me as best he could and said, without too much conviction, that it was probably harmless, but just to make sure it would be best if I went to see my doctor the following day, which I did.

My doctor looked very concerned as he examined me, and he arranged for me to see a Specialist the very same day. I remember how distressed the Specialist was when he told me I had a malignant tumour and would have to have my breast removed as soon as ever possible. I looked at him in terror and said: "That's out of the question — I'm expecting a baby in a few weeks time — there must be some mistake". He took my hand and gently said: "I'm sorry my dear, but I'm afraid there's no mistake and we must operate as soon as ever possible; we can't even afford to wait until after your baby is born. Try not to upset yourself too much and just pray that we have caught it in time to save both you and your unborn child. In the meantime, go home and get plenty of rest, and I'll make arrangements for you to be admitted to the Royal Infirmary within two or three days".

I broke the news to Robert, who was very distressed, but he did his best to keep calm for my sake, and also so that our little daughters would not fret any more than necessary.

The few days of waiting were the longest in the whole of my life, and although I did my best to hide my fears I honestly felt I was not strong enough to face up to an operation of this magnitude, and would surely die, leaving my darling husband to bring our daughters up on his own, with not even Mamma to help. I secretly decided that if there was a way out of going ahead with this operation then I would take it. Even if I only had a few more months to live, at least I could spend it with my family and make arrangements for their future, and apart from that I would not have to risk my unborn baby's life with the shock of the anaesthetic. Oh how I needed Mamma's shoulder to cry on.

The day after the 'verdict' my sister Patsy came to visit, and on seeing my distress she said: "Come on Marie — cheer up; let's go off to "The Spirits" — the name Mamma used to laughingly call the Spiritualist Church meetings. I had never been to one of these meetings before, but Patsy eventually talked me into it, and off we went.

On arrival at the Church we discovered that the meeting was already in progress and we could hear the congregation singing a hymn. Quietly we opened the door and crept inside, to find the Church full to capacity apart from two chairs on the back row that were still empty, as if waiting for us.

As soon as the hymn was over the Medium pointed directly at me and said: "There is a lady standing behind you with her hands on your shoulders and she tells me her name is Anne. She has dark hair and a longish nose and she's wearing spectacles. This lady is forcefully pushing you up a flight of stone steps, along a corridor, and into a large round room with lots of beds in it. She insists that you must go through with whatever is facing you, and wants you to know that all will be well". The Medium had described Mamma perfectly and had even given me her name, and there and then I decided I would be brave, and try to face the ordeal ahead with courage.

The following day I received the summons to attend the hospital, and although still afraid, Mamma's message, received through the Medium, had had a certain calming effect on me and I said goodbye to my little daughters, leaving them in Robert's care, and went off to the hospital, accompanied by my sister.

Patsy and I climbed the stone steps of the Royal Infirmary, in those days the finest hospital in Liverpool, and I was taken to a pre-med ward, where I was put to bed and made comfortable. Later that day I was wheeled into the operating theatre where I had a total mastectomy, and when I eventually opened my eyes after the operation I thought I was hallucinating because the ward I awoke in was a circular shape, exactly as Mamma had described it through the Medium. I had never before been in a round room of any kind and was comforted by the thought that Mamma had got it right so far and maybe all would be well for both me and my unborn child.

Marie aged 84

Two days after the operation my daughter was born — strong, healthy, and perfect in every way. We went home together about three weeks later, and although it took me some time to recover my strength it was obvious to everyone that the operation had been a complete success. That was 58 years ago and I never had a recurrence of the cancer which threatened my life. I often wondered if I would have been able to face up to it all without Mamma's guidance.

Looking back over my 84 years I have to admit they have been fraught with ill-health of one kind or another, having suffered a massive heart attack in my forties, followed by tuberculosis of the bladder and kidneys, to name but a few of the illnesses which beset me. In fact, whenever I do have to go into hospital, and the admission doctor asks what previous illnesses I have had, I always ask him, jokingly, if he has an hour or so to spare, for that's how long it would take for me to relate them.

One of my daughters often teases me, saying: "I'll take my hat off to whatever gets you into the next world Mum".

END